FAITH OUT LOUD

SEASONS

Discipleship Ministry Team
Ministry Council
Cumberland Presbyterian Church

January 2016

8207 Traditional Place
Cordova (Memphis), Tennessee 38016

MINISTRY COUNCIL
Cumberland Presbyterian Church

The Discipleship Ministry Team of the Ministry Council of the Cumberland Presbyterian Church is the successor organization to the Board of Christian Education of the Cumberland Presbyterian Church.

First Edition 2016

Published by The Discipleship Ministry Team, CPC
Memphis, Tennessee

ISBN-13: 978-0692625644
ISBN-10: 069262564X

We want to hear from you. Please send your comments about this curriculum to the Discipleship Ministry Team at faithoutloud@cumberland.org

OUR UNITED OUTREACH
Made Possible In Part By Your Tithe To Our United Outreach

Funded, in part, by your contributions to Our United Outreach.

SEASONS

LESSONS

FAITH OUT LOUD

ADVENT: GETTING READY FOR JESUS

BY JIMMY BYRD AND ANDY McCLUNG

SCRIPTURE
ISAIAH 2:4, ISAIAH 11:6, ISAIAH 35:1, ISAIAH 7:14

THEME
Advent is a time for preparation.

CONNECTING TO YOUR STUDENTS

Though each teen is unique, many times teens want to stand out from the crowd. But they don't want to be too different or stand out so much that it draws too much attention. It's a difficult balance to find and maintain. Perhaps a new hairstyle or hair color, bold eye makeup, or a pierced nostril? Maybe the key is that they want to stand out from the general population but not within their own teen subculture.

Though Christians are called to be in the world (after all, God made this place), the way we do things sometimes looks different. For Christians, the season of Advent leads up to Christmas day and New Year's. Advent begins the Christian liturgical year, so wishing others "Happy New Year" four Sundays before December 25 is appropriate, unusual, and a great way to start a conversation about Jesus.

We Christians have our own calendar. That's how different from the secular world we are called to be!

EXPLAINING THE TOPIC

You may have noticed that some people are now using "BCE" (Before Common Era) and "CE" (Common Era), rather than "BC" (Before Christ) and "AD" (Anno Domini/year of our Lord) to note dates. One can only assume that this is an effort to avoid the Christian references in both BC and AD. Ironically, though, BCE and CE are divided by the same event as BC and AD: the birth of Jesus. It's now fairly common knowledge that the BC/AD divide is actually off by several years, putting Jesus' probable birth around 6 to 4 years BC. Nevertheless, every time we write, note, or mention what year something happened, or what the current year is, we are referencing Jesus. It only makes sense; his was, after all, the most important birth ever.

On one hand, then, we can say that we already have a Christian calendar. It's called the Gregorian calendar, named after the pope during whose papacy it was made, and is the most-used calendar in the world. But there is another, more specifically, Christian calendar called the liturgical calendar that focuses on different elements of the Christian faith throughout the calendar year.

Since Jesus' was the most important birth ever, it would make sense for the liturgical calendar to begin with Christmas Day—but it doesn't. It doesn't, because we don't want to just plunge right in to important events. We should take time to prepare for them. Nobody goes to their prom without spending some time preparing for it. Nobody steps onto the field for the most important game of the season without preparing for it. Nobody who takes the birth of Jesus seriously should jump right into Christmas without first preparing for it. We call that time of preparation the season of Advent.

The word "advent" means "coming," and the season of Advent is a time to prepare for the Savior's arrival. There is a definite double meaning in Advent. We prepare to remember and celebrate Christ's first coming—the incarnation—and doing so hopefully makes us think and prepare for his second coming.

Note that most of this information pertains to the Western Church.
Some portions of the Eastern Church observe Advent differently.

Advent began as a three-week-long fast by persons planning to be baptized on Epiphany (January 6). This grew into a time of preparation for all Christians to participate in, focusing on preparing for the coming of Christ. But the focus was on Christ as judge, giving Advent a mood of penitence. Over the years, the time period expanded into four weeks, and the focus shifted to one of joy and hope. We emphasize how good God's coming kingdom will be, rather than how unworthy of it we are. We now save that for the season of Lent.

Nowadays, Advent always begins four Sundays before Christmas Day, giving us at least four weeks of Advent. Traditionally, a different theme is the focus of each week. These themes are not set in stone, however, and can be changed from year to year in the local congregation. They could be hope, peace, joy, and love; or expectation, preparation, repentance, and rejoicing; or the focus each week can be on a different Biblical character involved in preselected scripture readings.

What most folks envision when they think about Advent is the Advent wreath, which is full of symbolism. Advent wreaths can be used in family worship at home or in corporate worship at church. The wreath is a circle, representing eternity (no beginning, no end). A wreath made of greenery represents eternal life. Four candles are set in the circle, representing the four Sundays of Advent. A new candle is lit each Sunday until all four are burning. Usually these four candles are purple (or blue), but some traditions use a pink candle on the third week. Purple (or blue) is the color of royalty. In the middle of the wreath is a larger, white candle, which represents Christ. This candle is lit on Christmas day. Overall, this wreath represents an approaching event. You can see the passage of time in the diminishing candles, and time yet to come in the untouched candles. The light, representing goodness, increases as Christ's birth approaches.

Other elements of the corporate worship service also reflect the theme for each week: banners, stoles, altar cloths, hymns, etc. The liturgical color for Advent has traditionally been purple, but in recent years some congregations have shifted to using blue to distinguish between Advent and Lent.

Advent calendars are a fun way to observe Advent. They usually have some door or window to open for each day of Advent, behind which is an appropriate verse or image. Mass produced, secular Advent Calendars are available, but inaccurate. Having 25 "doors" to open, they're really just December, or "countdown to Christmas," calendars. While Advent has four Sundays each year, the actual number of days changes from year to year. Your best bet is to make your own Advent calendar each year.

The season of Advent ends when December 24 becomes December 25, and the season of Christmas begins.

THEOLOGICAL UNDERPINNINGS

The Cumberland Presbyterian Church does not require its individual congregations to follow any particular order of worship or to observe any particular season of the liturgical year. This means that some CP congregations are very focused on the liturgical seasons, some have never heard of them, and some fall somewhere in between. Traditionally, however, Presbyterianism gives attention to the liturgical year.

Non-liturgical congregations who are challenged to closely follow Advent practices for one year are likely to find a deeper meaning in the weeks preceding Christmas. Liturgically-minded congregations who are challenged to ignore Advent for one year are likely to have their interest in this ancient celebration rekindled the next year.

Advent hymns should focus on awaiting and preparing for the Savior's birth, not celebrating it. Thus "O Come, O Come, Emmanuel" is appropriate for Advent, but "Joy to the World" is not. Most hymnals do not have enough hymns appropriate for Advent, though. Worship planners often take the easy way out and use Christmas carols prematurely. It would be better to select other hymns that fit the week's theme, thereby giving new insight into those hymns.

C.S. Lewis wrote, "The central miracle asserted by Christians is the incarnation." Both the importance and impossibility of God becoming human cannot be overstated. Christmas, the incarnation and birth of Jesus, is an important event, and we take time to prepare for important events. The season of Advent is that time of preparation. While we are preparing to remember and celebrate Christ's first coming as Jesus, we're also thinking about his second coming. The four passages from Isaiah are used in the Advent liturgy and are understood to be prophecies which reveal the world Jesus showed us God intended—the world that will be when Christ returns.

APPLYING THE LESSON TO YOUR OWN LIFE

Recall an important event that you knew was coming, but you didn't prepare for. Now recall an important event that you knew was coming, and you did prepare for. Compare your enjoyment of the two events. Which involved more peace? Which involved more joy?

On which aspect does your pastor place more focus: the historical events of Jesus' life, or the spiritual meaning behind those events? Which are you more interested in? Which do you focus on more in your teaching?

Do you emphasize Advent in your home? Does your congregation emphasize Advent? Or do you/your congregation treat this season as a "countdown to Christmas?"

If your congregation does not use an Advent wreath, consider making one or asking session to purchase one. Check out the liturgy associated with lighting the candles in corporate worship found in The Book of Common Worship, published by the Cumberland Presbyterian Church and some other denominations.

ADVENT: GETTING READY FOR JESUS
BY JIMMY BYRD AND ANDY McCLUNG

SCRIPTURE
ISAIAH 2:4, ISAIAH 11:6, ISAIAH 35:1, ISAIAH 7:14

LEADER PREP

RESOURCE LIST
- Construction paper
- Markers, crayons
- Poster board
- Sheets of paper for each student
- Tape or glue
- Pencils or pens
- An Advent wreath with candles

BEFORE THE LESSON
Make sure your church has an Advent wreath you can borrow for the lesson. If they don't, they are easy to make. You can usually find an Advent wreath set at your local Christian bookstore. Or just simply put four purple or blue candles in a circle and one white candle in the middle.

Find Christmas music for Advent such as: "Come, Though Long Expected Jesus," or "O Come, O Come, Emmanuel."

The liturgical color for Advent is purple or blue. You may want to encourage your class to wear purple or blue for the day this lesson is taught. It can also be a good discussion starter if anyone asks them why they are dressed that way.

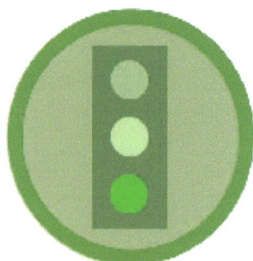

GET STARTED

GET STARTED (5 minutes)
SAY: Today we begin a six-lesson study on the church calendar or what is also called the liturgical calendar.

Go over the different liturgical holidays that you will be covering over the next six lessons: Advent, Christmas and Epiphany, Lent, Easter, Pentecost, and Ordinary Time.

SAY: Today we look at the season of Advent.

LISTEN UP

LISTEN UP (15 minutes)
Give each student a sheet of paper and a pencil or pen. Have students write down a list of at least ten things they do to get ready for Christmas. After everyone is finished, have them read aloud their lists. Be sure to take note of all the items that are the same, such as buying gifts, decorating the tree, etc.

ASK: Can anyone tell me what the season of Advent means?

ANSWER: To prepare for the arrival of the Christ child.

8

SAY: Advent begins four Sundays before Christmas day. These four weeks help us to prepare ourselves spiritually for the coming of the Messiah.

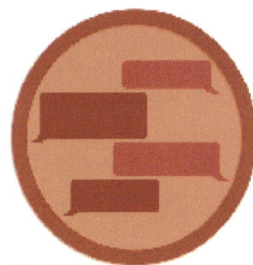

Have students look at their lists again from the beginning of this segment.

ASK: How many items on your list help you get ready spiritually for Christmas?

Give students a couple of minutes to discuss.

The Israelites had been preparing for the Messiah for many generations. Prophets like Isaiah had predicted signs to look for. Have students look up the following passages: Isaiah 2:4, Isaiah 11:6, Isaiah 35:1, and Isaiah 7:14. Have the students tell how each of these verses describes the changes that the Messiah will bring into the world.

If your church has an Advent wreath, set it up on a table in the classroom. You can also make your own Advent wreath with four purple or blue candles and one white candle, using the description on page 6, explaining to the students the meaning of lighting each candle. Make sure you light each one as you describe it.

NOW WHAT

NOW WHAT? (20 minutes)

Have the students make their own Advent calendars. Using pencils, crayons, markers, plain copy paper, construction paper, poster board, or whatever you think is best, let the students design their own calendars, beginning with the first Sunday in Advent and ending on Christmas Eve. Make sure you have a current calendar available to look at the accurate dates for this year.

Let the students be as creative as they want to be with their calendars. They can include scripture passages for each Sunday of Advent and/or for each day

of the week. They can include the name of a different person each day (a family member, friend, church member, etc.) that they want to pray for. They could also send a card, email, or text to the person they have listed on each day as well.

By making these calendars, the students are preparing themselves (and potentially others) for the coming of the Christ child. It helps the students focus on the deeper spiritual meaning of Christmas. Encourage the students to use the calendars during Advent. If they want, they could make this a family tradition.

While the class is making their Advent calendar, feel free to play some Advent music in the background.

The Discipleship Ministry Team develops a great Advent devotional book each year. If you have money in your budget, you may want to purchase one for each student in your group. The books usually cost about $3.50 each.

LIVE IT (5 minutes)
Let everyone show off their Advent calendar.

End with this prayer:
God of grace, we wait with anticipation for the coming of the Messiah. Prepare us as we wait. Prepare our hearts, our minds, and our souls. Do not let us get distracted. Fill us with excitement as we prepare to celebrate the coming of our Lord, Jesus Christ. Amen.

LIVE IT

NOTES

Resources used in compiling background information: <u>Liturgical Year: The Worship of God</u>, <u>Miracles</u> by C.S. Lewis. Pictures used: Advent by Christian Schirner - https://goo.gl/aACf27, Advent Calendar Box Templates by Tina D - https://goo.gl/aXL5dU, Christmas Due by Jannis Andrija Schnitzer - https://goo.gl/pPJM2t, Advent candles by John Taylor - https://goo.gl/8LYFWM

FAITH OUT LOUD

CHRISTMAS AND EPIPHANY
BY JIMMY BYRD AND ANDY McCLUNG

SCRIPTURE
LUKE 2:1-20, MATTHEW 2:1-12, JOHN 1:1-9

THEME
Christmas is a season, not just a day. Epiphany is its own special day. Celebrating these historical events points us toward eternity.

CONNECTING TO YOUR STUDENTS

Everybody loves Christmas. Really, it's been proven. A 2011 poll asked 2,462 US adults, "Thinking of all the holidays that occur during the calendar year, which one would you say is your favorite?" With no additional prompting, persons asked that question—both genders, multiple age groups (18-66+) and ethnicities—gave Christmas as the top answer.

If that same poll had asked participants to define "the Christmas season," most people probably would have said it starts around Thanksgiving and ends when Christmas day ends. This idea comes from retailers and marketers because, that's when all the ads, TV specials, and shopping happens. But we can only remain excited about something for so long. By the time Christmas actually gets here, many people are physically, emotionally, and financially worn out. The Church has an answer for this.

EXPLAINING THE TOPIC

When we observe Advent as a time of preparation and anticipation, saving the joyous celebration for Christmas, then both seasons are more meaningful. Christmas truly is a season, but not within the time frame the world tells us.

Christmas couldn't be just one day because there's absolutely no way we can adequately celebrate the most important birth in history in just one day. Remember that old song "The Twelve Days of Christmas?" Well, somebody didn't just randomly choose the number twelve because they wanted to write a really long song that's hard to remember; Christmas really is twelve days long. The season of Christmas begins December 25 and ends January 5. January 6 is another holy day called Epiphany.

Trivia: The claim that "The Twelve Days of Christmas" originated as a secret teaching tool by persecuted Roman Catholics in Britain, with each of the items mentioned in the song referring to a point of Catholic doctrine, is probably not entirely accurate and may even be completely false.

Some critics of Christianity have mockingly pointed out that there's no evidence that Jesus was born on December 25. Some of these critics even go so far as to call Christians ignorant or stupid for believing this. Well, the joke is on them: the Church has never claimed that Jesus was born on December 25. Celebrating his birth on a specific day and claiming to know the exact day of his birth are two very different things. (It is true, however, that some Christians oversimplify things by making "Happy Birthday, Jesus" cakes as part of their Christmas celebration, and some Christians may believe that Christmas is Jesus' true birthdate.)

More educated critics of Christianity like to point out that the Church "stole" the December 25 date from pagans who celebrated Saturnalia, a festival honoring the god Saturn, around this time. This is quite likely, but it was not a case of theft. God has always been in the business of taking common things and making them sacred. It's called redemption.

Some congregations have a Christmas Eve service, which includes readings of appropriate scripture passages interspersed with singing appropriate hymns. This is called a Service of Lessons and Carols. Some congregations include the celebration of Holy Communion in this service. Others have "come and go" Communion only.

The liturgical color for both Christmas and Epiphany is white, so the cloths on the pulpit and communion table, as well as the pastor's stole, should be white. White symbolizes both Christ and purity. The center candle of the Advent wreath, also white, is only to be lit during the Christmas season (December 25-January 5), but some congregations go ahead and light it for the Christmas Eve service.

In recent years some Christians have become more vocal in their complaints that secular culture has hijacked Christmas. They say we Christians need to "take back" this holy day. This mindset manifests itself, in part, in anger over greetings such as "Happy Holidays" rather than "Merry Christmas", and schools having "winter break instead of "Christmas break." This is actually not a new concern at all; it's just that with today's communication abilities, it's easier for these complaints to be heard far and wide. And while persons with this concern may seem to be overreacting, it is clear that in the U.S., Christmas has indeed been seriously commercialized. If you talk to the older generations, they'll likely recall a time when Christmas was much simpler; Christmas was more family oriented, children expected and received simpler gifts, and most everyone in town would be in church to at least acknowledge Jesus' birth as the reason for Christmas (even if they only attended church on Christmas and Easter). In the UK, a 2014 poll showed that a third of 10 to 13 year olds don't know that Christmas celebrates Jesus' birth. Half of the overall population says they celebrate Christmas, but Jesus' birth is irrelevant to their celebrations. Only 10% of adults polled could state four facts about Jesus' birth. (Many such religion-focused polls are done in the UK; far fewer are done in the U.S.) In 1954, a story by C.S. Lewis was published in the UK called "Xmas and Christmas." This entire story is in Lewis' book entitled <u>God in the Dock</u>, and it's summarized on page 15 under "Digging Deeper."

Epiphany is a one-day celebration, January 6. Since that date does not always fall on a Sunday, however, many congregations who observe Epiphany designate the closest Sunday morning worship service as Epiphany Sunday. This is the day we celebrate the magi/wise men finding the young Jesus and presenting their gifts. The birth of Jesus and the wise men's visit were two completely separate events by up to two full years. So all those nativity sets and works of art (not to mention church Christmas plays) with the shepherds and wise men gathered around Mary and Joseph looking down at Jesus in the manger...they're all historically inaccurate. The wise men weren't there.

Were there really three wise men? Find the answer in the
Faith Out Loud Lesson "That's Not in the Bible?!?"

THEOLOGICAL UNDERPINNINGS

Paying attention to, and even shaping our worship around the liturgical calendar may seem to be paying more attention to historical events than the eternal works of God. When observed properly, though, the liturgical calendar calls us to focus on the latter. The historical events ground God's eternal work in a specific place and time, making them real. If we treat them as reality, they then draw our consideration beyond space and time to eternity. Baby Jesus was born at a particular time in a particular place to a particular woman. Noting this makes us ask why this event is important to remember, and why it's worthy of celebration 2,000 years later. We conclude that this event forces us to consider the incarnation and exactly who the Messiah is. The visit of the wise men makes us ask why these Gentiles were honoring a Jewish baby as a king. We conclude that God became human to save the whole world, not just Israelites; God is more gracious than even those closest to him ever imagined.

The theological focus of Christmas is the incarnation—God becoming human in Jesus. This is an incredible testimony of God's love for us. Omnipotent, omniscient, omnipresent God voluntarily chose to lower himself to our level in order to save us from sin and death. God chose to put up with hunger, thirst, being sick, and much worse for our sake, when he didn't have to ever experience anything but being infinitely powerful and glorious God.

As for the feast of Saturnalia, redeeming and sanctifying a pagan celebration (and this was apparently an "anything goes" celebration) is a reflection of what God does to each person who accepts Christ. We are changed from worshiping false gods and seeking our own pleasure, sometimes at the expense of others, to worshiping the one true God and seeking his pleasure, which benefits everyone.

Epiphany is about much more than remembering the historical event of wise men visiting a small child. Their valuable gifts to him make us realize how valuable a gift Jesus was to the whole world, and how we are called to be gifts to the world as well. Epiphany reminds us that being Christian isn't only about getting into heaven after we die; it's equally about making this world as much like heaven as we possibly can before we die.

APPLYING THE LESSON TO YOUR OWN LIFE
Thinking of all the holidays that occur during the calendar year, which one would you say is your favorite? Do you know anybody who wouldn't answer with "Christmas?" If so, why wouldn't they? Of these three choices, which best describes you? A) I enjoy the religious Christmas stuff at church and the secular Christmas stuff elsewhere; B) I've found a comfortable blend that allows me to honor Christ, but doesn't offend anybody with other ideas about Christmas; C) No matter where I am, I'm all about Jesus throughout the Christmas season. Are you comfortable with this position? Do you think it pleases God? Do you have another stance on Christmas? Do you get tired of Christmas busyness before December 25 even arrives? Do groups in your church (choir, Sunday school classes, etc.) have Christmas parties during Advent? If so, consider focusing more on preparation during Advent and celebrating during Christmas.

DIGGING DEEPER
Here is a summary of "Xmas and Christmas," CS Lewis' speculation about what an ancient historian might observe upon finding himself in contemporary Britain during the month of December. It was published in "Time and Tide," December 4, 1954. A portion of the story can be found online at http://oxfordinklings.blogspot.com/2006/12/exmas.html. The historian records that a great festival is being celebrated. It is called "Xmas" and is marked by a lot of activity. People send one another cards with bright pictures. They give one another gifts, taking extreme care to ensure that everyone who gives them a gift receives back one of equal value. The marketplace is so besieged with activity that both the sellers and buyers become dismal and exhausted. The rush to prepare for Xmas is so tiring, in fact, that when the day itself actually arrives most people lie in bed until noon. Despite all this activity, the historian notes that the reason behind "Xmas" is unclear.

The historian also notes that a few of the people he observes do just the opposite of the masses. At the same time most are rushing toward Xmas, these few are preparing for another festival, which they call "Christmas." When Christmas arrives, these few arise early and journey to their temples where they gather around images of a woman with a newborn child being adored by shepherds and animals. The reason behind Christmas is perfectly clear to the historian.

JUST IN CASE
If a student asks where we get the actual name "Christmas," explain that it was originally "Christ Mass" back when the only denomination was Roman Catholic. The mass part is what they call their public worship services. "Mass" comes from a Latin word meaning "to send." Such services are called masses because worshipers are sent from them to serve God.

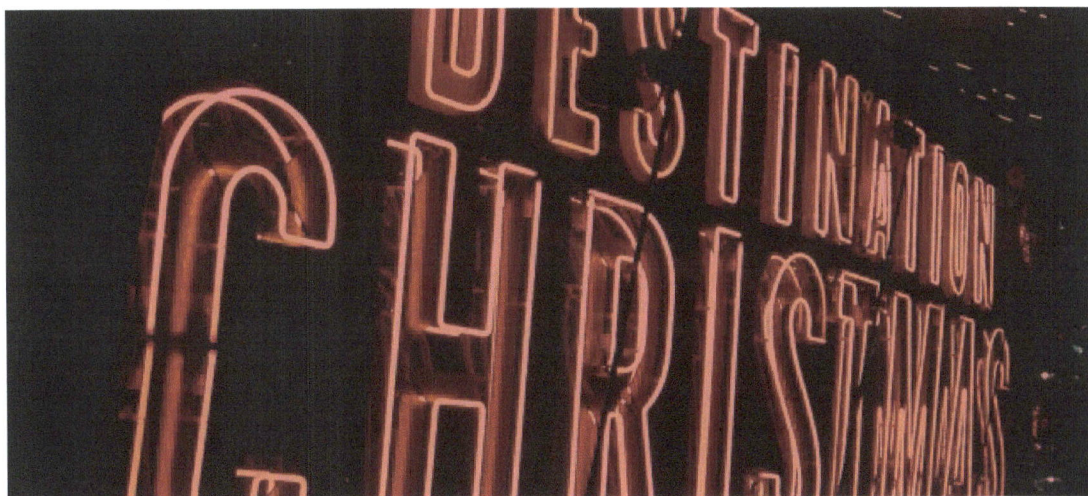

CHRISTMAS AND EPIPHANY
BY JIMMY BYRD AND ANDY McCLUNG

SCRIPTURE
LUKE 2:1-20, MATTHEW 2:1-12, JOHN 1:1-9

LEADER PREP

RESOURCE LIST
- Copies of "Best/Worst Gift Ever" at the end of this lesson

- Pens or pencils

- Manger or baby crib

- Flashlights or glow sticks—one for each person

- TV, DVD player, copy of "A Christmas Carol" DVD, copy of The Playbook - A Resource for Games and Other Group Related Activities by Roger Maness, Kenny Shackelford, and Dan Washburn

BEFORE LESSON

If your church has a manger, place it in your classroom. You can put some hay or straw in it. If you do not have a manger, you could use a baby crib in its place. Place small flashlights, flashlight key chains, or glow sticks in the manger, and cover them so the students do not see them. There needs to be one item per student, and these can be found at a dollar store.

If you chose to use the video clip from "A Christmas Carol," make sure you have it cued up for the lesson.

The liturgical color for Christmas and Epiphany is white. You may want to encourage your class to wear white for the day that this lesson is taught. It can also be a good discussion starter if anyone asks them why they are dressed that way.

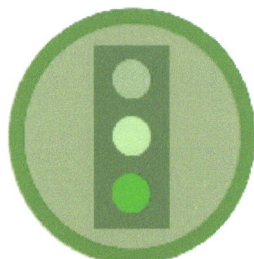

GET STARTED (15 minutes)
Option 1: Pass out the "Best/Worst Gift Ever" handout to the students. After everyone has filled out their sheets, give them time to discuss their answers.

Option 2: If you have a copy of The Playbook – A Resource for Games and Other Group Related Activities, by Roger Maness, Kenny Shackelford, and Dan Washburn, pages 39-41 have awesome Christmas puzzle games. You can make copies for each student. You can order this book from Cumberland Presbyterian resources and at Amazon.com.

GET STARTED

LISTEN UP (15 minutes)
SAY: For many, Christmas is their favorite holiday of the year. It is full of excitement and joy. In the church we sing Christmas songs, do Christmas plays, have Christmas parties, etc. Outside of church we are Christmas shopping, getting together with family we only see once a year, putting up lights, putting up a tree, etc. We can get so busy at Christmas that we miss the whole meaning of it!

LISTEN UP

SAY: Today we are going to slow down and think about what Christmas really means. Christmas is about receiving God's greatest gift, the Messiah. For centuries, the Israelites had been watching, waiting, and expecting a Savior. Finally, the promise of God had been fulfilled and a Savior was born. Jesus was born to save all humankind and to offer grace and forgiveness. On that special night he was the love of God wrapped up in clothes and laid in a manger.

Draw your students' attention to the manger in the room.

SAY: While I read from Luke 2:1-20, the story of the birth of Christ, I want you to look at the manger and think about what Mary and Joseph went through to bring Jesus into this world. Think about the journey they made from Nazareth to Bethlehem. Think about their frustration at not finding a home in Bethlehem to stay the night. Were they nervous or panicking trying to find a place to stay as Mary was about to give birth? Think about the terror the shepherds experienced as the angel appeared to them. Think about the shepherds' excitement as they were the first ones to see the Messiah.

Read from Luke 2:1-20, and then give students a chance to respond with their thoughts.

NOW WHAT

NOW WHAT? (10 minutes)
SAY: Remember the movie "A Christmas Carol," based on the book by Charles Dickens? At the end of the movie, Ebenezer Scrooge wakes up from his restless night of being visited by three spirits that were trying to help him change from his wicked ways. Mr. Scrooge had indeed changed and went from hating Christmas to loving and cherishing it. When he woke up, though, he was afraid he had missed Christmas all together. He was disappointed that he had wasted another Christmas thinking only of himself and not others.

(If you have the movie "A Christmas Carol," you can show the class
this scene from the end of the movie. Pretty much any version
will do, but I always prefer the George C. Scott version.)

SAY: Little did Mr. Scrooge know, and maybe some of you, that Christmas actually lasts longer than one day! The season of Christmas goes from December 25 – January 5. (Refer to the background info on page 13.)

SAY: January 6th is a special day to celebrate the Wise Men, or Magi, coming to see Jesus and presenting him gifts. This event likely did not take place when Jesus was a baby but perhaps nearly two years later.

Have someone read Matthew 2:1-12.

DISCUSSION QUESTIONS

SAY: With this in mind, it should give us a whole new perspective on Christmas. God gave us the greatest gift in God's son, Jesus Christ.

ASK: What can you do to spread God's love with these extra days of Christmas?

LIVE IT (5 minutes)

SAY: For some people, Christmas is one of the hardest times of the year. Some people don't have a family to get together with at Christmas. Some have lost loved ones, and it makes it harder to be joyful at Christmas. Some do not have the money to buy gifts for their children or each other. This is a great place where you can share the gift of God's love at Christmas. This Christmas season, ask God to place someone or some people on your heart to share the love of Jesus with. Are there shut-ins or widows in our church who would love some company? Maybe there are families who cannot afford to buy Christmas gifts. We could help buy gifts for them or take up a collection. If there is someone that is grieving over the death of a loved one, let them know they are loved. Send them a text, an email, or a card each day of the Christmas season. There are so many ways to let people know about the love and grace of the Savior born over 2000 years ago.

Read John 1:1-9.

After reading from the passage, give each student one of the flashlights or glow sticks. Tell them that they are to be a light that shines in the darkness, and this light can remind them to let the light of Christ shine through them. Remind them that their light can shine all year long, not just at Christmas time.

Close in prayer.

NOTES

Resources used in compiling background information: dailymail.co.uk, dictionary.com, harrisinteractive.com, Liturgical Year: The Worship of God, Westminster Dictionary of Theological Terms, Xmas and Christmas, by C.S. Lewis, The Playbook - A Resource for Games and Other Group Related Activities by Roger Maness, Kenny Shackelford, and Dan Washburn. Pictures used: Star by Susanne Nilsson - https://goo.gl/aACf27

BEST & WORST GIFT EVER

List three of the worst Christmas gifts you have ever received.

1 _____

2 _____

3 _____

List three of the best Christmas gifts you have ever received.

1 _____

2 _____

3 _____

FAITH OUT LOUD

LENT
BY JIMMY BYRD AND ANDY McCLUNG

SCRIPTURE
GENESIS 3:19, MATTHEW 21:1-11, MARK 14:22-25,
MARK 15:22-25

THEME
Lent is a time of self-reflection, self-denial, and self-discipline, all of which draw us beyond ourselves to focus more fully on Christ.

CONNECTING TO YOUR STUDENTS

Most teens know about some aspects of Mardi Gras. However, unless they've grown up in a congregation and/or a home where Lent is observed, they may not know why Mardi Gras (Fat Tuesday) occurs when it does. Mardi Gras, a time of self-indulgence and debauchery, immediately precedes Lent, a time of self-denial and moderation. The over-indulgences of Mardi Gras began as a way to "get it out of your system" before attempting the self-discipline of Lent. It's doubtful this ever really worked, and it's questionable if those who now participate in wild Mardi Gras celebrations intend to undertake any spiritual discipline during Lent.

Few teens will seek out opportunities on their own to engage in serious self-reflection, self-denial, confession, and repentance. But a lot of teens who somehow find themselves in situations to engage in these very practices come out on the other side amazed at how spiritually uplifted they are. Lent is the perfect time for this.

EXPLAINING THE TOPIC

The season of Lent is the 40 days before Easter, not including Sundays. The word "Lent" is from the Middle English "lente," which meant "spring," and "lente" comes from the Old English "lengten" meaning "to lengthen," as in "The daylight lengthens in spring." Plants coming out of their winter dormancy have always made humans think of new life.

It was customary in the early church for persons wishing to join the Church to make a profession of faith and be baptized on Easter Day. Because becoming a Christian and joining the Church was (and still is) a big deal, it took some preparation (and still should). The candidates for membership would fast, pray, confess, repent, and study scripture for several weeks before Easter to prepare for that day. Believers already in the Church joined them in fasting and praying the final week before Easter, using it as a time for self-reflection, confession, and repentance so that they might be fully ready to participate in the celebration of the resurrection on Easter.

Lent begins on Ash Wednesday. The "Ash" comes from the practice of using ashes to remind us that we will, sooner or later, die. "Ashes to ashes, dust to dust." Traditionally the pastor uses ashes to make a smudge or a cross on the forehead of Christians while saying "[person's name], remember that you are dust, and to dust you shall return." This may sound rather morbid, but it's meant to affirm that life is a gift of God, and because of sin this life will indeed end. There's no getting around it. There's no use ignoring it. Death is inevitable. Ash Wednesday recognizes this, but not in a morbid way. Ashes are a sign of brokenness and mourning as we acknowledge our own waywardness and seek God's everlasting forgiveness in preparation for Easter. Many Christians find great meaning in fasting during Lent. Fasting is voluntarily giving up something that we don't need in order to focus more fully on God. Some people fast from specific foods, others from specific behaviors or activities. The thing fasted from should be decided upon after seeking God's guidance through prayer. Fasting is done Monday through Saturday only. Sunday is the Lord's Day; all attention should be on God, so on Sunday we feast instead of fast.

It is an old tradition not to say or sing "hallelujah" during Lent. "Hallelujah" means "praise the Lord." We still praise God during Lent, but something about fasting from this word makes it much more significant to say on Easter Day. In addition to giving up (fasting from) something during Lent, the tradition is to also take up something. Bible study, charitable giving, service to others, and extra prayer time are possibilities. The thing fasted from and the thing taken up can even be linked. For example: you give up junk food for Lent and give the money you would have been spent on it to the local food bank.

The final week of Lent is Holy Week, which corresponds with the final week of Jesus' earthly life. Palm Sunday is the day we remember Jesus' triumphal entry into Jerusalem. This was the day the Jewish people treated Jesus like the king he was, making him a "red" carpet from their clothes and pulling off palm tree branches to wave in the air (Matthew 21:1-11, Mark 11:1-11, Luke 19:28-38, John 12:12-15). Many congregations get palm leaves for folks to wave in worship on Palm Sunday. Thursday of Holy Week is Maundy Thursday. "Maundy" comes from the Latin word "mandatum." This is the day Jesus instituted the Lord's Supper and gave his disciples the commandment—or mandate—to love one another as he has loved them (John 13:34-35). He demonstrated this through his washing of their feet. Friday of Holy Week is Good Friday, derived from "God's Friday." It's the day Jesus was crucified, died, and was buried in a borrowed tomb.

A meaningful and traditional practice is to save the palm leaves from palm Sunday, let them dry, and them burn them to produce ashes for the next Ash Wednesday.

Special worship services are very appropriate on Maundy Thursday and Good Friday. The Thursday service can include a celebration of the Lord's Supper with an emphasis on Christian service. The tradition is to strip the worship space at the end of this service, taking away all the cloths, flowers, plants, Bibles, candles, etc. to leave the space as bare as possible. Crosses and other ornaments that can't be removed are covered with black cloth. Seeing this reminds us of Jesus' utter loneliness and desolation as he prepared himself to endure arrest, torture, and execution. The Good Friday service, occurring in this stark setting, is quite somber as it focuses on Jesus' crucifixion and death. It usually includes reading appropriate scriptures, singing appropriate hymns, and prayers. The worship space can be made progressively darker as the service progresses, ending in darkness to represent Jesus being in the grave. This service should end with everyone leaving in mournful silence.

The liturgical color for all of Lent is purple, which represents Jesus' royalty...plus it's dark.

THEOLOGICAL UNDERPINNINGS
In recent years, some folks noticed that a lot of Christians were at church on Palm Sunday celebrating Jesus' triumphal entry, and then back in church on Easter Sunday celebrating the resurrection. It didn't seem right for so many people to be skipping over all the anguish, pain, and suffering in between these two celebrations. Since Easter isn't the time to focus on the cross, but rather on the empty tomb, they turned to Palm Sunday. Some congregations now call it Passion Sunday and focus on the cross instead of the triumphal entry. So in a way, we contemporary Christians have joined with the Pharisees in Luke 19:39, trying to diminish the one moment Jesus was treated as he deserved.

"Passion" comes from the Latin word meaning "suffering" and refers to Jesus' spiritual and physical suffering before and during the crucifixion.

Fasting is a spiritual practice. It's mentioned several times in scripture and is always accompanied by prayer. We don't fast for any other reason other than to make ourselves more spiritually healthy by stepping away from things with the potential to get between us and God. Part of fasting is focusing on Christ's suffering whenever you feel the desire for the food or activity you're fasting from.

The resurrection of Jesus is the most important event in history, an event that affects every human being who will ever exist. Observing Lent helps us prepare to celebrate that event, draws us closer to Christ in his suffering, and makes us better at living Christ-like lives.

APPLYING THE LESSON TO YOUR OWN LIFE
If you've ever fasted from something for Lent (or some other period of time), spend some time recalling and reflecting on that experience. Ponder over why you did or did not find it spiritually beneficial.

If you've never fasted from some food or behavior, try it for a day or two in the week before you lead this lesson. Record the experience in a journal and consider reading some of it to the class.

Does your congregation have an Ash Wednesday service? If so, does it include the imposition of ashes? One CP pastor, when proposing an Ash Wednesday service to the session, was told, "That's not Christian, that's Catholic!" How would you respond to such a remark?

If your congregation does not have Maundy Thursday or Good Friday services, ask your session why not. Many congregations don't because they don't expect many people to show up for the services. Is that a valid reason? Do you think it's fair to Christ to go from the "mountaintop" of Palm Sunday to the "mountaintop" of Easter Sunday without passing through the valley in between?

JUST IN CASE

No matter how meaningful the special worship services that happen inside the church are, the community outside the building can't see them. One way to share publicly the observance of Lent is to utilize an outdoor cross, even if it means erecting one specifically for Lent. A purple cloth can be draped on the cross throughout Lent, palm leaves can be affixed to it on Palm Sunday, the cloth switched to black on Good Friday, and then white on Easter Day. Plus, fresh flowers can be added to the palm leaves on Easter. One CP minister was once surprised to see a purple-draped cross outside a particular church building during Lent because it was of a non-liturgical denomination. The purple cloth stayed through Good Friday, Easter, and several months afterwards. Apparently they weren't being liturgical after all, but just thought it looked nice.

LENT
BY JIMMY BYRD AND ANDY McCLUNG

SCRIPTURE
GENESIS 3:19, MATTHEW 21:1-11, MARK 14:22-25, MARK 15:22-25

RESOURCE LIST
- Loaf of bread and grape juice
- A black light (optional)
- Lint rollers for each student (can be found at dollar store)
- Make a copy of the instructions for the different stations found at the end of the lesson.
- A cross
- Palm branch

LEADER PREP

BEFORE THE LESSON
Set up four stations in your classroom or in an area where you will not disturb anyone. Each station is described in the NOW WHAT section of this lesson. It would be a good idea to have your pastor bless the bread and juice before using it in the lesson.

The liturgical color for Lent is purple. Black is also used for Good Friday. You may want to encourage your class to wear black for the day that this lesson is taught. It can also be a good discussion starter if anyone asks them why they are dressed that way.

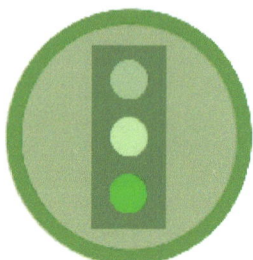

GET STARTED (5 minutes)
OPTION 1: Pass out lint rollers to each student. Give them one minute to roll all over their shirts and pants to see how much lint they can collect.

OPTION 2: Turn off the lights in the room and shine a black light on each person to show how much lint we actually have on our clothes.

OPTION 3: This is kind of gross but very easy and cheap. Have everyone stick a finger in their bellybutton and see how much lint they can pull out.

GET STARTED

After completing one of the options above, ask the following question to the students: Were you surprised at how much or how little lint you found?

Give a minute for discussion.

SAY: The lint, like our sin, can be invisible to us until something makes us notice it.

LISTEN UP (15 minutes)
Take time to go over the background information on Lent from pages 21-23.

SAY: The season of Lent has nothing to do with the kind of lint you find on your clothes, in the dryer, or in your belly button. It's even spelled differently. The season of Lent does have to do with noticing our sin and shortcomings in being a follower of Christ.

LISTEN UP

SAY: Advent is the season of preparation for Christmas; Lent is the season of preparation for Easter. Lent takes place 40 days before Easter and does not include Sundays, because Sunday is the Lord's Day—a "little Easter"—when we feast rather than fast. It begins on Ash Wednesday. Some churches have an Ash Wednesday service, where they put ashes on people's foreheads as a sign of repentance.

During the 40 days of Lent, people commonly give up something, or fast from something. Some give up sweets, soft drinks, TV, music, Facebook, etc. It's important to give up something that will actually be a sacrifice, not something you won't care about.

Give each student a copy of the handout found at the end of this session. Have them fill in the answers, and then take some time to discuss their answers.

Our CP resources also has a book called Live Lent—Devotionals for Lent that can be purchased for $3.50 plus shipping. These would be great books for the students to use during Lent to deepen their spiritual awareness of the meaning of Lent.

NOW WHAT? (20 minutes)

SAY: Holy Week is an important time that takes place during the season of Lent. It is the week leading up to Easter. It begins with Palm Sunday, remembering Jesus' triumphant entry into Jerusalem. Holy Week covers the last days of Jesus' life and includes the Last Supper, his crucifixion, and his entombment.

NOW WHAT

If you have room in your meeting place, set up four individual stations. At the first station, have a copy of "The Palm Branch" handout along with a palm branch. At the second station,

have a copy of "The Holy Communion" handout along with a loaf of bread and a cup of grape juice. At the third station, have a copy of "The Basin and Towel" handout along with a basin of water and a wash cloth or towel. At the fourth station, have a copy of "The Cross" handout along with a standing cross.
Have students pair up and form small groups to go to each station. One group can start at station one, while another can start at station two and so on.

If you do not have enough room for four stations, you can set up everything on one table and have everyone do each activity together. Make sure that the students understand that this is a serious activity, and no one needs to joke or kid around.

A very meaningful activity to do during Holy Week is to set up "Stations of the Cross." There are many more stations that you can include in addition to these four. Each station describes a different aspect of Jesus' final hours. A good resource for this and many other Lenten activities is Destination Easter, by Kathy Hershman and Kaylea Hutson.

LIVE IT (5 minutes)
After everyone has finished with the stations, gather the group together to quickly discuss their thoughts on what they experienced. Ask students how they felt while doing the stations, and what they may have learned about Lent.

End in prayer.

LIVE IT

NOTES

Resources used in compiling background information: Liturgical Year: The Worship of God, Westminster Dictionary of Theological Terms , Destination Easter by Kathy Hershman and Kaylea Hutson. Pictures used: Prayer Beads by Omer Unlu - https://goo.gl/GDrwyw, Bread and Wine by khrawlings - https://goo.gl/xiHfWy, Mary Magdalene by Charles Clegg - https://goo.gl/zAvZ1v, Palm by Stephen Cummings - https://goo.gl/u4RvoG, Princessehof - Detail Martavaan by Michele Ahin - https://goo.gl/a9BLtL, Communion by Evan Courtney - https://goo.gl/iQq9gu, Storm clouds over war cross, Wytschaete cemetery by R/DV/RS - https://goo.gl/e53feF, The Granite Cross by Tobias Lindman - https://goo.gl/nKYUWq

When they had come near Jerusalem and had reached Bethpage, at the Mount of Olives, Jesus sent two disciples, saying to them, "Go into the village ahead of you, and immediately you will find a donkey tied, and a colt with her; untie them and bring them to me. If anyone says anything to you, just say this, 'The Lord needs them.' And he will send them immediately. This took place to fulfill what had been spoken through the prophet, saying, "Tell the daughter of Zion, Look, your king is coming to you, humble, and mounted on a donkey, and on a colt, the foal of a donkey."

The disciples went and did as Jesus had directed them; they brought the donkey and the colt, and put their cloaks on them, and he sat on them. A very large crowd spread their cloaks on the road, and others cut branches from the trees and spread them on the road. The crowds that went ahead of him and that followed were shouting.

"Hosanna to the Son of David! Blessed is the one who comes in the name of the Lord! Hosanna in the highest heaven!"

When he entered Jerusalem, the whole city was in turmoil asking, "Who is this?" The crowds were saying, "This is the prophet Jesus from Nazareth in Galilee."

(Matthew 21:1-11, NRSV)

Pick up the palm branch and hold it in your hand. Wave it in front of you. Imagine being in the crowd that day and watching Jesus come by.

Would you be waving the palm branch, placing it on the road in front of him, and shouting Hosanna in the highest? What do you think it would have felt like to have been there in that moment?

Jesus horrified the disciples by washing their feet. This was something only a servant would do, not a rabbi and definitely not the Son of God. But Jesus was teaching the disciples a valuable lesson. He wanted them to understand the importance of serving others. The disciples were far from perfect and some of them already had big egos. Jesus brought them down a few notches by washing their feet. It was a humbling experience.

Now before the festival of the Passover, Jesus knew that his hour had come to depart from this world and go to the Father. Having loved his own who were in the world, he loved them to the end. The devil had already put it into the heart of Judas son of Simon Iscariot to betray him. And during supper Jesus, knowing that the Father had given all things into his hands, and that he had come from God and was going to God, got up from the table, took off his outer robe, and tied a towel around himself. Then he poured water into a basin and began to wash the disciples' feet and to wipe them with the towel that was tied around him. He came to Simon Peter, who said to him, "Lord, are you going to wash my feet?" Jesus answered, "You do not know now what I am doing, but later you will understand." Peter said to him, "You will never wash my feet." Jesus answered, "Unless I wash you, you have no share with me." Simon Peter said to him, "Lord, not my feet only but also my hands and my head!" Jesus said to him, "One who has bathed does not need to wash, except for the feet, but is entirely clean. And you are clean, though not all of you." For he knew who was to betray him; for this reason he said, "Not all of you are clean."

After he had washed their feet, had put on his robe, and had returned to the table, he said to them, "Do you know what I have done to you? You call me Teacher and Lord—and you are right, for that is what I am. So if I, your Lord and Teacher, have washed your feet, you also ought to wash one another's feet. For I have set you an example, that you also should do as I have done to you. Very truly, I tell you, servants are not greater than their master, nor are messengers greater than the one who sent them. If you know these things, you are blessed if you do them."

(John 13:1-17, NRSV)

Turn to your partner and use the wash cloth to wash their hands. Think about this scripture and about how Jesus humbled himself in service. Think of ways you might need to humble yourself as you serve others and God. Each of you, take turns washing each other's hands. Pray for opportunities to serve others.

THE BASIN AND TOWEL
STATION TWO

While they were eating, he took a loaf of bread, and after blessing it he broke it, gave it to them, and said, "Take; this is my body." Then he took a cup, and after giving thanks he gave it to them, and all of them drank from it. He said to them, "This is my blood of the covenant, which is poured out for many. Truly I tell you, I will never again drink of the fruit of the vine until the day when I drink it new in the kingdom of God." (Mark 14:22-25, NRSV)

Have you ever thought about what it must have been like for Jesus to have this last meal with his disciples, his friends? He wanted them to remember the sacrifice that he was making. He let the bread represent how his body would be broken. He let the wine represent his blood that would be poured out because of beatings and the cross.

When we eat of the bread and drink from the cup, we remember the sacrifice of Jesus. He suffered and died to forgive us and to offer us eternal life with him.

As you tear off a piece of the bread, dip it in the cup. As you taste the bread and the juice, remember what Jesus did for you.

Then they brought Jesus to the place called Golgotha (which means the place of skull). And they offered him wine mixed with myrrh; but he did not take it. And they crucified him, and divided his clothes among them, casting lots to decide what each should take. It was nine o'clock in the morning when they crucified him.

(Mark 15:22-25, NRSV)

The cross is the most famous symbol in Christianity. When we look at it, we are reminded of suffering and pain. As Christians, when we look at the cross, we are also reminded of love and hope. Jesus gave up his life in an act of love to forgive us of our sins. He gave us hope in eternal life through the pardon of the man crucified beside him. Jesus told the man, "Truly I tell you, today you will be with me in paradise." (Luke 23:43, NRSV)

Take time right now to silently pray for someone you know who is not a follower of Jesus, or for someone who is struggling with their faith. Maybe that person is you. Ask God to help you experience the love and forgiveness of Jesus Christ.

The cross should humble us and remind us that being a follower of Christ is not always easy. Many people around the world are being persecuted today for following Jesus.

Take time right now to silently pray for those who are suffering and being persecuted.

THE CROSS
STATION FOUR

FAITH OUT LOUD

EASTER
BY JIMMY BYRD AND ANDY McCLUNG

SCRIPTURE
MATTHEW 28:1-10, MARK 16:1-8, LUKE 24:1-12, JOHN 20:1-18

THEME
Easter is a season, and it's the most important one of them.

CONNECTING TO YOUR STUDENTS

Most people playing a word association game ("I'll say a word, and you say the first word that pops into your mind") would probably respond to "Easter" with "egg," "basket," or maybe "lily." Probably few would say anything religious. And why should they? The typical American Easter experience for kids is waking to baskets full of candy and gifts left by the Easter Bunny, putting on new clothes, going to church for an hour or two, hunting for plastic eggs somewhere, having a special meal, and then coming home to eat more of that candy, add those new clothes to their regular rotation, and play with those gifts for months. The religious part of this celebration is neither the part with the most time devoted to it, nor the part most likely to be recorded and photographed. It may even seem like the least important part of the day. This is sad because for Christians, the religious element of Easter is the most important part—not just the day, the whole year.

EXPLAINING THE TOPIC

The world tries to tell us that Easter is just one day, but according to the liturgical calendar, Easter is a season. As with Christmas, what Easter represents is impossible to adequately celebrate in one day, or even twelve days. The season of Easter lasts seven entire weeks (50 days).

The date of Easter is not fixed to a particular day of the year, but it is fixed to a particular day of the week. Thus, the actual date of Easter Day changes from year to year, but it's always on a Sunday. This was decided long ago by church leaders at the Council of Nicea in A.D. 325. Jesus' crucifixion and resurrection happened around the time of the Jewish Passover, which can occur on any day of the week. The Council of Nicea wanted to ensure that Easter maintained ties with Passover while also celebrating it on the day of the resurrection. So they decided Easter Day is the first Sunday after the first full moon occurring on, or after, March 21, the spring equinox. Thus, Easter Sunday can occur from March 22 all the way to April 25.

Some critics of Christianity like to say that Christians are ignorant of the fact that our celebration of Easter is really just a conglomeration of whitewashed pagan rituals. As with Christmas, though, the Church knew what it was doing. Almost every culture did indeed have some kind of pagan fertility ritual held in the spring. The hope of such rituals was to entice the proper god to provide a good harvest. As the Church spread into places with such rituals, it redeemed them, shifting the focus from appeasing false gods to praising the one true God. Imagine this as the Church's way of approaching participants of another religion without saying, "You've got it all wrong. Reject your gods and let me tell you about the true God," and instead saying, "You're right, there is a god of the harvest, and a god of the sea, and a god of the air. And guess what—they're all the same god! There's one God, and much bigger and better than you ever imagined. Let me tell you what all he's done. He humbled himself to become human, then died for all humankind, and then he conquered death."

One pagan goddess was Ishtar, called by many, similar sounding names in different cultures. Say it out loud and you'll hear how it sounds a lot like "Easter." Ishtar may be the one whom God is angry about people honoring in Jeremiah 7:16-18. Symbols of Easter include eggs, flowers, and a bunny. Eggs were used in pagan rituals because they easily represent fertility and new life. They were hung in pagan temples and supposedly colored with the blood of human sacrifices in some cultures. Flowers typically bloom in spring and are probably symbolic thereof in every culture. The rabbit has always been known to be quite prolific when it comes to fertility; when spring arrives, so do lots of new bunnies (and other animals).

> An egg is part of the contemporary Passover meal. It is displayed to commemorate the similar offering ancient Jews made in the temple for Passover. It's later eaten to symbolize mourning over the temple's destruction.

Some Christian groups refuse to celebrate Easter because of all this pagan symbolism. Some who refuse say that the resurrection should be celebrated every day and not just on Easter. What they, and those critics of Christianity, don't seem to understand is that the Church has never denied all the pagan stuff. It should be noted, however, that most of the criticized symbols (eggs, flowers, bunny) are part of the secular Easter celebration and not officially part of the Church's celebration. The Church's celebration focuses on the resurrection of Christ, and what it means both for humankind and all of creation. In the Church's celebration, Easter symbols become more than symbols, they become pictures of truth: an empty tomb, hope, assurance. Many congregations do, however, adopt the secular aspects of Easter celebrations seemingly with no thought to their pagan origins.

Some Christians are concerned with how secularized and commercialized Easter has become in the U.S. In 2015, Americans spent $14.6 billion on Easter, $2.1 billion of which was for candy alone. When polled, only 67% of U.S. adults called Easter a religious holiday, and only 42% were specific enough to say it's about Jesus' resurrection. That's sad, because Easter is all about Jesus' resurrection!

Worship during the Easter season should be celebratory. The celebration of Easter can be a more joyous moment when it comes after self-reflection, self-denial, and the self-sacrificing spiritual practices of Lent. Shouting or singing "hallelujah" after weeks of refraining makes the act feel more meaningful. Eating that particular food or engaging in that particular behavior after fasting from it makes it much better and properly ordered in importance.

The liturgical color for Easter is white, symbolizing Christ's purity. A special Christ candle can be lit during worship. All scripture readings, liturgy, and hymns should be about resurrection. Holy Week is the time to focus on the cross and Jesus' blood and suffering on our behalf; Easter is all about celebrating the resurrection.

THEOLOGICAL UNDERPINNINGS
Jesus' resurrection changed everything. No longer did death have the last say. The power of the resurrection was almost immediately apparent, too. While tons of people came out to witness Jesus' miracles, only twelve (now eleven) were with him every moment of his ministry. These eleven ended up changing the world, but it didn't seem like that was going to be the case at first. The Bible is clear that the crucifixion caught them by surprise. Even though Jesus had warned them about it, they just didn't get it. They were without their leader. They were hiding, afraid that they'd be arrested next. They didn't know what to do or where to go. For them, it seemed the whole thing was over; if Jesus was dead, then he must not have been the Messiah after all. But after they learned of the resurrection, they changed. Just a few weeks later they had reconnected with and/or gathered new believers so that there were about 120 serious followers (Acts 1:15). Shortly after that, at Pentecost, thousands more joined them. Since then, the Church has grown to more than two billion people and has done an amazing amount of ministry in Christ's name. And it all started with the resurrection showing eleven scared people that if God can reverse death itself, then nothing is impossible for God.

Jesus' death was to pay for our sins. His resurrection was to give us the hope and the chance to share in his resurrection after our own deaths.

The connection between Passover and Easter is no accident. Passover was a commemoration of the day God's judgment against the Egyptians passed over the homes of the Israelites (Exodus 12:12, 23) and put things in motion to set them free from slavery to Egypt. Easter celebrates all of creation (Confession of Faith 1.15) being set free from slavery to sin and death.

APPLYING THE LESSON TO YOUR OWN LIFE

Do you think of Easter as a day or a season? If the former, consider ways to expand your concept of Easter. Ask your church's session to figure out ways to emphasize Easter as a season.

Does your congregation hold an egg hunt? If so, what's the theological justification for it? Is it held before Easter, when we're still supposed to be in the somberness of Lent, or is it part of the Easter celebration? Compare how much money, effort, time, and thought you spend on secular Easter stuff and on religious Easter stuff. If you're heavy on the secular stuff, make a plan to shift your focus next Easter. Consider giving to your church some of the money normally spent on candy, etc.

Consider finding somewhere you can attend a Seder meal. ("Seder" = "order." It's the ritual surrounding the Passover meal.) This would not be a regular Jewish Seder, but one planned and prepared so that Gentiles could be present. Many Christians find that this experience deepens their appreciation of the Lord's Supper.

JUST IN CASE

If a student is interested in how the dates of Passover and Easter correspond, add to the above information that our calendar (called the Gregorian calendar) is based on the solar year (the 365.25 days it takes for Earth to rotate around the sun), but the Jewish calendar uses the lunar year, 12 cycles of 29 or 30 days (354.37 in total, requiring frequent adjustments to match the solar year.) Each month begins with the new moon. This puts the full moon halfway through each month. The Jewish year begins in late September/early October with Rash Hashanah. The Passover is always on the 14th day of the month Nisan, during the full moon. The full moon that determines Easter's date is usually the full moon in the sky for Passover.

EASTER
BY JIMMY BYRD AND ANDY McCLUNG

SCRIPTURE
MATTHEW 28:1-10, MARK 16:1-8, LUKE 24:1-12, JOHN 20:1-18

LEADER PREP

RESOURCES
• Plastic eggs filled with a piece of candy, one empty plastic egg for each student

• Dry erase board or newsprint and dry erase markers

• Pen or pencils

• Bible for each student

• Opitional video clip http://goo.gl/u4B81y

BEFORE THE LESSON
If you want to show the video clip in the Listen Up section, make sure you have a laptop or tablet and an internet connection.

The liturgical color for Easter is white. You may want to encourage your class to wear white for the day that this lesson it taught. It can also be a good discussion starter if anyone asks them why they are dressed that way.

GET STARTED (5 minutes)
Give everyone a plastic egg. All of the eggs should have a piece of candy in them except for one. Don't let the students open their eggs until everyone has received one. The student with the empty egg will obviously be surprised and feel short changed because the rest of the class received candy.

SAY: Easter has become a holiday about eggs, candy, and bunnies.

GET STARTED

DISCUSSION QUESTIONS

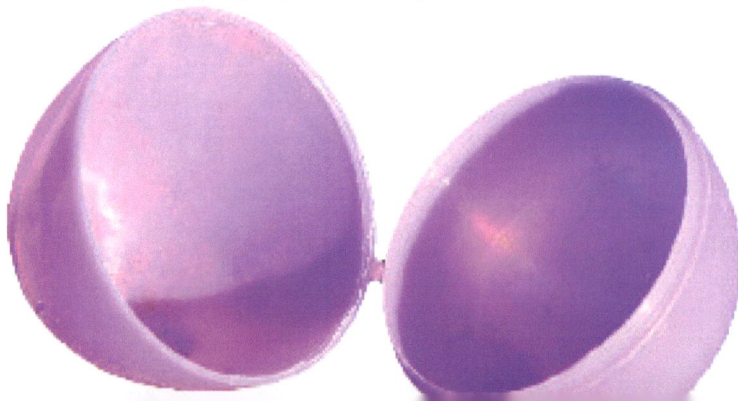

ASK: Why would I give you an egg that was empty?

SAY: It's to remind you of the real reason of Easter: the emptiness of the tomb.

Give the student who had the empty egg a piece of candy.

LISTEN UP (15 minutes)

SAY: Easter is the most important season in our Christian faith. If Jesus had not been resurrected from the tomb, there would be no hope for our resurrection. Unfortunately, like Christmas, the real meaning of Easter gets bogged down by many other distractions.

ASK: Can you name all the things associated with the holiday of Easter?

DISCUSSION QUESTIONS

Write down answers on a dry erase board or newsprint paper for everyone to see.

ASK: Now how many of these things actually have to do with the resurrection of Jesus, and how many are secular things?

Go over the background information about the origins of the secular symbols of Easter (the egg, bunny, and flowers) with the students.

Here is a video clip you can use: http://goo.gl/u4B81y
The clip shows where some of our secular Easter traditions have come from.

ASK: Are these items and traditions used at Easter hurting the meaning of Easter, or can they be used in good ways to enhance Easter? Give time for discussion.

SAY: The main goal is that we do not lose the real meaning of Easter. If you want to have an egg hunt or decorate eggs, that is OK. Just don't lose focus. Once Easter is reduced to only chocolate bunnies and hiding eggs, the good news of the resurrection is lost. For some people today, Easter has nothing to do with the resurrection of Jesus. According to a poll in 2015, only 67% of U.S. adults called Easter a religious holiday.

NOW WHAT? (20 minutes)

All four gospels give details about the resurrection of Jesus. Some of the details differ in each account, but overall they point to the fact that Jesus did indeed rise from the dead.

Divide your class into four groups. Give each group one of the following passages of scripture: Matthew 28:1-10, Mark 16:1-8, Luke 24:1-12, or John 20:1-18. Give each group a chance to read over the passage. Once they have read it, have them act out the passage. Let them be as creative as they want, using appropriate props from around the room. One person can narrate the scripture as it is being acted out, or they can simply act it out without a reading. After everyone has finished, take a few minutes for discussion.

ASK: Which of the four versions of the gospel do you prefer? Why?

ASK: What are some of the differences between the four versions?

ASK: How are the four versions similar?

DISCUSSION QUESTIONS

SAY: Even though there are small differences in the details of the story, the main point is still the same, Jesus defeated death and the grave was empty. Resurrection from death is real through Jesus Christ!

The differences in the four accounts of the resurrection story actually make the historical fact of the event more plausible. Chances are that a fabricated story would have all the same details and plot points. Many eyewitnesses of the same car accident would all remember the same crash, but the details they remembered, or decided to share, would be different.

LIVE IT (5-10 minutes)
ASK: Does anyone know why the date of Easter changes every year?

ANSWER: It is the first Sunday after the first full moon that occurs on or after March 21st. (See background on page 33 for more information.)

LIVE IT   **SAY**: In our Christian calendar, Easter is actually celebrated for fifty days, not just one day. That is seven weeks dedicated to the celebration of Jesus overcoming death.

ASK: What are some things you can do to celebrate fifty days of Easter?

ASK: What are things that we as a class can do over the seven weeks of the Easter season to spread the good news of the resurrection?

DISCUSSION QUESTIONS

Take all the suggestions into consideration, have someone write down the ideas, and devise a plan for the next Easter season to use those ideas to promote the resurrection.

Close in prayer.

Does your church plan a Sunrise Service on Easter morning? If so, what do you usually do? Would it be possible for your class to help lead the service? Some churches have breakfast after the Sunrise Service. If your class is unable to lead the service, maybe they could help serve the breakfast.

A children's Sunday school teacher in our church orders butterfly cocoons every year during Lent. She sets up a small container with the cocoons, and the kids get to watch them open as it gets closer to Easter. She orders them at www.insectlore.com.

NOTES

Resources used in compiling background information: askmoses.com, Guess What I Discovered on the Way to Church? by Diane Otto, oikoumene.org, rayfowler.org, statisticbrain.com, Westminster Dictionary of Theological Terms, http://www.history.com/topics/holidays/history-of-easter/videos/bet-you-didnt-know-easter-traditions, www.insectlore.com Pictures used: Sunrise at Mt. Haleakalā by Dustin A. Lewis - https://goo.gl/meUOWo, Unknown - http://goo.gl/2XMkZl

FAITH OUT LOUD

PENTECOST
BY JIMMY BYRD AND ANDY McCLUNG

SCRIPTURE
ACTS 2:1-42, JOHN 8:1-11, LUKE 22:47-53, MATTHEW 5:43-48

THEME
The importance of Pentecost is that the Holy Spirit is at work in the Church.

CONNECTING TO YOUR STUDENTS

The word "Pentecost" may make your students think of a Pentecostal church and the particularly animated style of worship there. Some Cumberland Presbyterian congregations are far more energetic in their worship style than others, but it's unlikely that your congregation's worship services are as consistently lively as those at Pentecostal churches. If your students are aware of the typical Pentecostal style of worship, then they might associate celebrating Pentecost with speaking in tongues, falling on the floor, dancing during the service, and jumping around in worship. Your students may find such activities curious, appealing, humorous, or scary. Make a clear distinction, then, between 1) the mainstream worship tradition of recognizing the historical account of Pentecost, honoring what God did there and continues to do in the Church, and 2) the high-energy, Pentecostal worship style. This lesson focuses not on human style in worship, but the activity of the Holy Spirit on that Day of Pentecost in Acts Chapter 2, and what it still means to us today.

EXPLAINING THE TOPIC

The number seven is particularly meaningful in Judaism. It represents completion and perfection. Its significance is increased by multiplication. Remember when Peter tried to impress Jesus by suggesting we should forgive fellow believers seven times, but then Jesus said to multiply that seven by seventy more times (Matthew 18:21-22)? Jesus wasn't giving a specific number, but rather using the Jewish idea of seven multiplied to perfection or completion to say that Christians should never stop forgiving one another. So a period of seven weeks of seven days each, then, would have been significantly meaningful.

At the beginning of Passover, Jews would offer a small amount of grain to God. Forty-nine days later they would complete the grain harvesting. The next day, the 50th day, they would feast and celebrate. They were celebrating God's taking something small—a bit of grain—and transforming it into something big—an entire crop of grains. The ties with Passover were clear, so this was also a celebration of deliverance from slavery. This day was called the Festival of Weeks, since it was held after seven weeks, or The Fifty Days. The celebration was one of gratitude, thanking God for providing them nourishment, something that sustains life. Like Passover, this was one of the Jewish holy days on which every Jewish adult male was supposed to make a pilgrimage to Jerusalem. So on Pentecost there would be Jews from many different places all together in one place.

The Greek translation of the Hebrew words for "fifty days" is where we get the English word "Pentecost." So Pentecost was a Jewish holy day long before what we read about in Acts. Many Christians regard Pentecost as the "birthday" of the church, because this is when the Jesus followers were blessed by God, started to get organized, and understood what their purpose was.

> Acts 2:1-42, is a really long scripture reading with many hard-to-pronounce words, but use the whole thing in class, as this was a pivotal moment in the life of the church. (It's okay for students to stumble and giggle over the hard words.)

Besides Acts 2, there are two other Biblical mentions of Pentecost in the New Testament: Acts 20:16, and 1 Corinthians 16:8. Neither of these references adds to our understanding of the celebration itself, but their very presence does affirm that the early church recognized this day's significance and observed it as a holy day.

Pentecost is also called Whitsunday in some places. Pentecost is unique on the liturgical calendar. It can either be celebrated as a single day or as a season. If celebrated as a season, it lasts several months, concluding only when Advent begins the new liturgical year. Pentecost as a season emphasizes that the Holy Spirit is continually working through the church. When celebrated as a single day, the day of Pentecost, the remaining time is observed as Ordinary Time, which is where we spend most of our lives – in the ordinary days, doing ordinary things.

Pentecost worship should be triumphant and joyful and should emphasize the Holy Spirit. This is the day God transformed the church from 120 uncertain and unsure people to more than 3,000 people who were ready to expand the kingdom of God.

Red is the liturgical color for the Day of Pentecost. It symbolizes the fire of the Holy Spirit that rested upon the gathered believers at the first Christian Pentecost. There are lots of creative things a congregation can do in worship on the day of Pentecost. You can ask everyone to wear something red that Sunday; have red, helium balloons tied to the pews/chairs at various heights so they appear to rest over worshipers' heads; string various lengths of red, orange, and yellow streamers from the light fixtures or ceiling to represent flames; hang wind chimes where the moving air from the climate control system will make them move; set up powerful fans to create a mighty wind at certain points in the service. Some pastors, instead of preparing a sermon for Pentecost, will stand up and say something like, "We're all together in one place. We believe the Holy Spirit is present among us. I'm going to sit down and be quiet. If the Spirit moves you to stand up and say, sing, do, or pray something, then follow that guidance." If such things are new to the congregation, even a small change can have a big impact.

Doing new or strange things, however, should never be the focus of worship. The focus of worship is reserved for God alone.

THEOLOGICAL UNDERPINNINGS
Jesus told his disciples that once he was gone, God would send the Holy Spirit to guide them (John 14:15-30, 15:26-27, 16:5-15). They didn't understand what he meant, but God, as always, kept his promise. It seems as if those disciples were caught completely by surprise when the Holy Spirit poured over them at Pentecost. From this we learn that we do not control the Holy Spirit, and we do not have to completely understand the Holy Spirit to follow the Spirit's guidance.

It was no accident that God chose to pour out the Holy Spirit on Pentecost. As millions of Jews celebrated how God took a small bit of grain and transformed it into a huge harvest, God, by the power of the Holy Spirit, was also transforming the small handful of Christ-followers (about 120 people) into a much bigger family. As all those Jews were thanking God for nourishing them physically with that grain, God was revealing how he would spiritually nourish everybody who accepts Jesus as Messiah/Savior. As those Jews remembered how God had saved their ancestors from death at the first Passover, God was revealing how everyone who accepts Jesus would be saved from death.

Some scholars say that Pentecost is to Easter, what God giving Moses the Law was to the Passover. In other words, in Exodus God freed the Israelites from certain death and then told them the best possible way to live: by following the Law. Then in the New Testament, God freed all creation from certain death through the crucifixion and resurrection and then told them to best way to live: by following the guidance of the Holy Spirit. This is reflected in our Confession of Faith 4.01. In fact, our Confession of Faith has a lot to say about the Holy Spirit. It is through the work of the Spirit that God calls us to repentance, gives us the faith to respond to that call, justifies us before God, regenerates us into new persons in Christ, sanctifies us, and gives us the assurance that we are indeed saved. All this is evident in the events of Pentecost and the continuing work of God in our lives. So "Pentecostal" may not be in our denomination's name or any of our congregations' names, but the importance of Pentecost is clearly in our theology.

APPLYING THE LESSON TO YOUR OWN LIFE
What comes to your mind when you hear the word "Pentecost?" What do you think about typical Pentecostal worship? What factors, experiences, biases, and prejudices shape your thoughts on that matter? Recall a time you experienced the presence and/or activity of the Holy Spirit. What was it like?

What was going on at the time? Were you in corporate worship or alone? What was the result of that experience? Consider sharing some of your reflections with the class. Does your congregation make a big deal out of Pentecost? If not, speak to your session about paying more attention to this holy day. Consider offering to set up one of the creative ideas above for the next day of Pentecost. How do you think the congregation would respond to such things? Write down your expectations and compare them with what happens. Do you refer to the Holy Spirit as "he," "she," or "it?" Why do you choose that pronoun? How do you react when others use a different pronoun? Why?

JUST IN CASE

One of your students may ask about speaking in tongues. If so, explain that there seem to be three types of this. In one type, the Holy Spirit gives a person the ability to speak in a language (tongue) that is not his or her own, but is spoken by some other culture. A less-immediate version of this would be someone having the God-given gift/ability to learn foreign languages easily. Such people might put this gift to use as international missionaries, social workers for immigrants, or Bible interpreters. Another type would be the Holy Spirit spontaneously causing a person to be able to speak in an unknown language and simultaneously giving someone else in the same place the ability to interpret that language. Such occurrences are considered to be prophetic, messages from God. The third type of speaking in tongues is when a worshiper begins speaking in an unknown language (tongue), and no one else is able to translate. This person is said to be speaking directly to God in a special prayer language. Much of this is addressed by the Apostle Paul in 1 Corinthians 14. Some Cumberland Presbyterians believe in the latter two types of tongues, and some do not. Officially we do not say speaking in tongues is wrong or false or evil. What disturbs many who do not worship this way, though, is when those who do speak in tongues say that this is the penultimate mark of salvation or faith; in other words, those who have not spoken in tongues have not received the Holy Spirit and therefore are not truly saved.

PENTECOST

BY JIMMY BYRD AND ANDY McCLUNG

SCRIPTURE
ACTS 2:1-42 JOHN 8:1-11, LUKE 22:47-53, MATTHEW 5:43-48

RESOURCE LIST
- Red balloons – one for each student
- "The Story of Pentecost" at the end of the lesson
- One or two fans
- Crayons, markers, colored pencils
- Paper to draw on

LEADER PREP

BEFORE THE LESSON
Encourage everyone to wear red for this lesson, since the liturgical color for Pentecost is red, and it also represents the holy tongues of fire.

GET STARTED (5 minutes)
Give each student a red balloon and have them blow them up and tie them. Give them a black marker if they would like to draw flames on their balloons. Pass out copies of the handout "The Story of Pentecost" for each student. Read the instructions and then read out loud the "The Story of Pentecost."

GET STARTED

LISTEN UP (20 minutes)
ASK: Can anyone explain the difference to me between Pentecost and Pentecostal?

ANSWER: Pentecost is celebrating the outpouring of the Holy Spirit upon the apostles and the early believers, as well as the beginning of the Church. Pentecostal is a type of worship that usually involves speaking in tongues, shouting, dancing, jumping around, and falling down on the floor.

LISTEN UP

ASK: Has anyone ever been to a Pentecostal church before? If so, what was it like?

SAY: In the Cumberland Presbyterian Church we typically do not speak in tongues or shout in worship. In some CP churches, it's really hard just to get an "Amen!" There is nothing wrong with that style of worship, but we usually do not worship that way.

DISCUSSION QUESTIONS

SAY: We do, however, celebrate the day of Pentecost, which follows 50 days after Easter Sunday. Pentecost ends the Jewish Festival of Weeks that celebrated the harvesting of grain. Traditionally, the Festival of Weeks ends the time of Passover. For Christians today, Pentecost ends the season of Easter. (For deeper information on the history of Pentecost, refer to the background infoon pages 41-42.)

SAY: The amazing things that happened on the day of Pentecost helped lay the foundation for the Church. The number of followers that day grew from 120 to over 3000 because of the power of the Holy Spirit.

OPTION 1: Do a dramatic reading of Acts 2:1-42.

*Have fans blowing in the background to represent the rushing wind of the Holy Spirit.

Have students follow along on their handout sheets and encourage them to participate in the actions.

You can read the whole passage, or you can pick a volunteer or volunteers to read it.

OPTION 2: Have students draw a picture of the scene at Pentecost, while you read the Scripture passage.

Provide crayons, markers, colored pencils, and paper to draw on. After the reading is finished, and the class is finished with their drawings, let them show off their work. Their pictures could be used during your next Pentecost worship service.

NOW WHAT? (15 minutes)

SAY: Now that we have heard about the outpouring of the Holy Spirit upon the apostles at Pentecost, what does that mean for us today? What does the Bible say about the Holy Spirit? There are many passages referring to the Holy Spirit, but we are going to look at six specific ones.

Have students look up the following passages. You can assign a passage to an individual or group, depending on the size of your class. After a passage is read, have the whole group discuss the role of the Holy Spirit in the particular passage.

Romans 8:26, 1 Corinthians 6:19, Romans 8:6, Galatians 5:22, Titus 3:5, Ephesians 1:13.

LIVE IT (5 minutes)

Close with this prayer:

Your Spirit, present from the beginning of beginnings, present in the message of the prophets, present in provision for your people, present in the life and words of Jesus, present in the Cross and crucifixion, present in the lives of the apostles, present in the church that you empower. Your Spirit, the presence of God in hearts and lives! Amen.

Read more at: http://www.faithandworship.com/prayers_Pentecost.htm#ixzz3glF7rZRO
Under Creative Commons License: Attribution

Each year at Pentecost, the Cumberland Presbyterian Church takes up an offering to support our missionaries. The offering is called the Stott/Wallace Offering, named after Buddy and Beverly Stott and Boyce and Beth Wallace. One hundred percent of the offering goes directly to fund our Cumberland Presbyterian missionaries around the world. Encourage your students to save their spare change or budget money each month to contribute to this special offering on Pentecost Sunday.

NOTES

Resources used in compiling background information: The Liturgical Year: The Worship of God, The New Bible Dictionary, The New Westminster Dictionary of Liturgy and Worship, Westminster Dictionary of Theological Terms, http://www.faithandworship.com/prayers_Pentecost.htm#ixzz3glF7rZRO Pictures used: 32679 Pentecost Decorations First Presbyterian Church May 27, 2012, photo by Bill McChesney -

https://goo.gl/gbmGD9

THE STORY OF PENTECOST

- **When the tongues of fire are mentioned, raise your balloons above your heads.**

- **When Peter's name is mentioned shout, "ROCK ON!" since Peter is referred to as the Rock.**

- **When David's name is mentioned, make a slingshot motion with your hands, refering to David killing Goliath.**

- **When you hear Jesus, Lord, or Messiah, make a cross with two fingers.**

- **When you hear the Holy Spirit mentioned, make a whooshing sound.**

THE STORY OF PENTECOST

[1] When the day of Pentecost had come, they were all together in one place. [2] And suddenly from heaven there came a sound like the rush of a violent wind, and it filled the entire house where they were sitting. [3] Divided tongues, as of fire, appeared among them, and a tongue rested on each of them. [4] All of them were filled with the Holy Spirit and began to speak in other languages, as the Spirit gave them ability.

[5] Now there were devout Jews from every nation under heaven living in Jerusalem. [6] And at this sound the crowd gathered and was bewildered, because each one heard them speaking in the native language of each. [7] Amazed and astonished, they asked, "Are not all these who are speaking Galileans? [8] And how is it that we hear, each of us, in our own native language? [9] Parthians, Medes, Elamites, and residents of Mesopotamia, Judea and Cappadocia, Pontus and Asia, [10] Phrygia and Pamphylia, Egypt and the parts of Libya belonging to Cyrene, and visitors from Rome, both Jews and proselytes, [11] Cretans and

Arabs—in our own languages we hear them speaking about God's deeds of power." [12] All were amazed and perplexed, saying to one another, "What does this mean?" [13] But others sneered and said, "They are filled with new wine." [14] But Peter, standing with the eleven, raised his voice and addressed them, "Men of Judea and all who live in Jerusalem, let this be known to you, and listen to what I say. [15] Indeed, these are not drunk, as you suppose, for it is only nine o'clock in the morning. [16] No, this is what was spoken through the prophet Joel:

[17] 'In the last days it will be, God declares, that I will pour out my Spirit upon all flesh, and your sons and your daughters shall prophesy, and your young men shall see visions, and your old men shall dream dreams. [18] Even upon my slaves, both men and women, in those days I will pour out my Spirit; and they shall prophesy. [19] And I will show portents in the heaven above and signs on the earth below, blood, and fire, and smoky mist. [20] The sun shall be turned to darkness and the moon to blood, before the coming of the Lord's great and glorious day. [21] Then everyone who calls on the name of the Lord shall be saved.' [22] "You that are Israelites, listen to what I have to say: Jesus of Nazareth, a man attested to you by God with deeds of power, wonders, and signs that God did through him among you, as you yourselves know— [23] this man, handed over to you according to the definite plan and foreknowledge of God, you crucified and killed by the hands of those outside the law. [24] But God raised him up, having freed him from death, because it was

impossible for him to be held in its power. [25] For David says concerning him, 'I saw the Lord always before me, for he is at my right hand so that I will not be shaken; [26] therefore my heart was glad, and my tongue rejoiced; moreover my flesh will live in hope. [27] For you will not abandon my soul to Hades, or let your Holy One experience corruption. [28] You have made known to me the ways of life; you will make me full of gladness with your presence.'

[29] "Fellow Israelites, I may say to you confidently of our ancestor David that he both died and was buried, and his tomb is with us to this day. [30] Since he was a prophet, he knew that God had sworn with an oath to him that he would put one of his descendants on his throne. [31] Foreseeing this, David spoke of the resurrection of the Messiah, saying, 'He was not abandoned to Hades, nor did his flesh experience corruption.' [32] This Jesus God raised up, and of that all of us are witnesses. [33] Being therefore exalted at the right hand of God, and having received from the Father the promise of the Holy Spirit, he has poured out this that you both see and hear. [34] For David did not ascend into the heavens, but he himself says, 'The Lord said to my Lord, "Sit at my right hand,[35] until I make your enemies your footstool."' [36] Therefore let the entire house of Israel know with certainty that God has made him both Lord and Messiah, this Jesus whom you crucified."

[37] Now when they heard this, they were cut to the heart and said to Peter and to the other apostles, "Brothers, what should we do?" [38] Peter said to them, "Repent, and be baptized every one of you in the name of Jesus Christ so that your sins may be forgiven; and you will receive the gift of the Holy Spirit. [39] For the promise is for you, for your children, and for all who are far away, everyone whom the Lord our God calls to him." [40] And he testified with many other arguments and exhorted them, saying, "Save yourselves from this corrupt generation." [41] So those who welcomed his message were baptized, and that day about three thousand persons were added. [42] They devoted themselves to the apostles' teaching and fellowship, to the breaking of bread and the prayers.

(ACTS 2:1-42, NRSV)

FAITH OUT LOUD

ORDINARY TIME DOESN'T HAVE TO BE SO ORDINARY

BY JIMMY BYRD AND ANDY McCLUNG

SCRIPTURE
MATTHEW 3:13-17, MATTHEW 17:1-13, JOHN 18:33-37, REVELATION 1:4-8, MATTHEW 28:18-20, ROMANS 12:1

THEME
On the liturgical calendar, as in life, there are plenty of ordinary days. But even some of those can become extraordinary.

CONNECTING TO YOUR STUDENTS

Your students may remember a time when they were younger, when they wistfully said something like, "I wish every day could be my birthday." Hopefully they've come to realize that if their birthday, an infrequent and special event, happened every day, then their special day wouldn't be special at all. It would be quite common...as common as, say, almost every other day.

By this point in this series of lessons, your students may be thinking that there are so many special days and seasons in the liturgical year that none of them are really special at all. The difference between the liturgical calendar and the birthday–every–day dilemma, however, is that each of the special holy days and seasons we've covered in this series so far has a different focus.

Sure, the average person would get tired of celebrating his or her own birthday every day, but nobody gets tired of celebrating a different holiday every month or so. Yes, they're each special, but they're each special for a different reason. But still, even those days wouldn't be special if every single day of the year was special. We have to have some ordinary time to even be able to recognize the special times.

EXPLAINING THE TOPIC

One way of looking at the liturgical calendar is to include two periods each year called Ordinary Time. One of these periods occurs between Epiphany and Lent, and the other between Pentecost and the beginning of the new liturgical year at Advent.

> The lectionary is a prescribed set of scripture readings—one each from the Old Testament, Psalms, Gospels, and Epistles—with a common theme for each Sunday of the liturgical year, including special days and seasons. "Lectionary" comes from the Latin word for "to read."

Ordinary Time is those periods of time in which no major holy days or seasons occur. This is where we spend most of our Sundays. This is when our focus is not on a special celebration but on worshiping and serving God in our ordinary lives. The funny thing is, because God is who God is, we often end up finding the extraordinary in Ordinary Time.

We Christians have so much to celebrate and be thankful for, though. Even during Ordinary Time we have several special things that have been given special days of recognition. They are, in chronological order:

Baptism of the Lord is the Sunday following whichever Sunday Epiphany (January 6) is recognized. On this day we remember, celebrate, and give thanks for Jesus' baptism, administered by John the Baptizer with the water of the Jordan River. This is when Jesus was anointed by the Holy Spirit and declared to be "my son" by God. It's also when his public ministry began. Baptism of the Lord is a great day to schedule baptisms, because it's a day for us to think of our own baptism and remember that we are God's adopted children, called to do ministry ourselves.

Transfiguration Sunday occurs the Sunday before Ash Wednesday and focuses on the time Jesus' true glory was glimpsed. Jesus was transfigured in the view of some of the disciples and met with glorified Moses and Elijah, who represented, respectively, the Law and the Prophets, all of which had pointed to the Messiah for generations. On this day we are to ponder the true glory of the Savior.

Trinity Sunday is the Sunday following Pentecost, and is rare in that it's based on a theological concept rather than a historical event. Because God as a Holy Trinity is impossible for the human mind to understand, this day should focus not on trying to explain the Trinity, but celebrating, adoring, and praising the Trinity as part of the mystery (or unknowable nature) of God. But do note that just because we're incapable of understanding the Trinity doesn't mean we shouldn't try.

All Saints' Day is not an official holy day for Protestants. The actual date is November 1, but since that only occasionally falls on a Sunday, it can be recognized on the Sunday closest to this date. In the Roman Catholic Church, this day is to remember all those departed Christians who have been granted sainthood, and November 2 is All Souls' Day to remember all believers who have died. Protestants believe in the sainthood of all believers, so we use All Saints' Day to celebrate all believers who have passed from this life. This is a very meaningful time of worship when observed properly. The congregation members can speak aloud the names of departed loved ones, and a special prayer of thanks can be offered for them. Or a worship leader can read the names of church members who have died in the past year and offer a prayer of thanks, which becomes particularly meaningful when those sitting through this worship service year after year know that their names will one day be read in a future All Saints' service.

Christ the King, also called Reign of Christ, is the final Sunday of the liturgical year, the Sunday before Advent begins. By promising to live as Jesus showed us and follow the guidance of the Holy Spirit, we each make Christ our Lord, but God made Christ Lord of all. This day centers on Christ as king, or ruler, of the universe. This day falls at the end of the liturgical year because Christ is the Alpha and Omega, the beginning and the end. In Christ, all things began (John 1:1-4), and in Christ all things will be fulfilled. No matter how strong evil's hold is on this world now, in the end, Christ will be victorious and will rule all. Since the concept of "king" is both archaic and foreign to contemporary Christians in North America, it might be a good idea to explore what Jews and earlier Christians envisioned when they thought of Christ as a king.

The liturgical color for Sundays of Ordinary Time is green, but for these special days it's white.

THEOLOGICAL UNDERPINNINGS
When we look at the life of Jesus, we see peaks and valleys, times of joy and times of sorrow. He went from the thrill of being born to running for his life from Herod. He went from the glory of his baptism to the physical and spiritual struggle of being tempted in the wilderness. He went from the joy of healing the Gerasene demoniac to the irritation of being run off by the guy's neighbors. He went from the high of the triumphal entry into Jerusalem to the low of being arrested and beaten. We even get to see some of his ordinary days, sitting around teaching the disciples. (Most ordinary days for anyone tend not to be recorded for posterity, though.) Our highs and lows may not be as important as Jesus' (even though they seem pretty earth-shaking to us at the time), but isn't that the rhythm that we all go through? One day we're on a spiritual high—just back from a good retreat, a week at camp, or an awesome mission trip—and a few days later somebody we love gets sick, or our boyfriend/girlfriend wants to break up. And mixed in there are plenty of ordinary days.

This rhythm of highs, lows, and ordinary times is reflected in the liturgical year. We get the joy and excitement of Advent, Christmas, Epiphany, and Easter. We get the somberness of Lent and the sadness of Good Friday. And we get plenty of Ordinary Time in between, which is a good thing, because when we're in the middle of those highs or lows, we're usually just in the moment. It's in the ordinary times that we have the leisure to reflect on, to ponder the meaning of, to consider the significance of, and to examine the lessons to be learned from all of those highs and lows. So thank God for Ordinary Time.

APPLYING THE LESSON TO YOUR OWN LIFE
Based on a typical year, try to put percentages on the following: "highs" in your life, "lows" in your life, and ordinary days in your life. Really spend some time on this and do your figuring carefully.

Are you surprised by your results? Optimists initially would probably say that they have more highs in their life, while pessimists initially would probably say that they have more lows. Regardless of our disposition, high and low days tend to stand out in our memories, but statistically speaking most of us have far more ordinary days than anything else.

Recall a time you really needed some ordinary time (a break from highs and lows). Now recall a time you experienced God change something ordinary into something extraordinary, maybe even something sacred. What was the result of that experience? Consider sharing your reflections with the class.
Of the special days within ordinary time covered in this lesson, which one are you most drawn to? Which one interests you the least? Does your congregation pay attention to these? If not, how might doing so enrich the life and ministry of your church?

JUST IN CASE

One of your students who has been present for all or most of this lesson series may ask why holidays such as New Year's Day, Mother's Day, Father's Day, Independence Day, and Thanksgiving weren't mentioned. Simply put, these are not on the liturgical calendar because they are not Christian holy days, but rather secular holidays. Some congregations treat them as equally important to the liturgical holy days the Church has recognized and celebrated for many centuries (or even as more important), but in truth, they're not. In the big picture, such days of special recognition are recently created and observed only in the U.S. One of the great things about being part of the Church Universal is that when we gather for worship, we're tapping in to and connecting with something that is far bigger and more important than our own community, state, or nation, transcending borders to join with our fellow Christians around the world. Even in a country as great as the U.S., a nation with a God-centered foundation and heritage, patriotism to country and faithfulness to God are not the same thing. Christians hold citizenship first and foremost in the kingdom of God, and our worship should reflect that.

ORDINARY TIME DOESN'T HAVE TO BE SO ORDINARY

BY JIMMY BYRD AND ANDY McCLUNG

SCRIPTURE
MATTHEW 3:13-17, MATTHEW 17:1-13, JOHN 18:33-37, REVELATION 1:4-8, MATTHEW 28:18-20, ROMANS 12:1

RESOURCE LIST

LEADER PREP

- Copies of "Best Day Ever" handout for each student

- Pencils or pens

- Copies of "Story of My Life" handout for each student (If you choose Option #1)

- The movie The Hobbit

- TV/DVD player or computer/projector

- Basic notebook for each student for NOW WHAT activity

BEFORE THE LESSON
Make copies of the two handouts so each student can have one. Have the beginning of the movie The Hobbit cued to show how ordinary Bilbo Baggins is. The YouTube link is here: https://www.youtube.com/watch?v=_LUPCclOULk

The liturgical color for Ordinary Time is green. You may want to encourage your class to wear green for the day that this lesson is taught. It can also be a good discussion starter if anyone asks them why they are dressed that way.

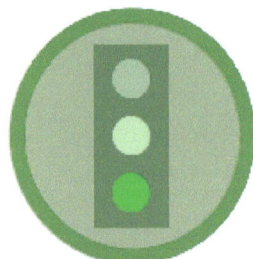

GET STARTED (10 minutes)
Pass out the "Best Day Ever" handout to each student. Give them five minutes to fill it out. Have each student share their moments from the sheet.

ASK: Which of the three moments on the sheet were the hardest to fill out: Best Day, Most Embarrassing Day, or Most Ordinary Day?

LISTEN UP (15 minutes)
SAY: Did you realize that most of our days are spent in the time between extraordinary events? We all have special days and seasons that stand out to us like our birthday, Christmas, vacation time, church camp, mission trips, etc. We have days that stand out as good days and days that stand out as bad, but most of our days are ordinary or routine. Most of our time is spent in between the big events.

Have each student describe a typical day in their lives.

ASK: Does anyone see any similarities? Differences?

OPTION 1: Give each student a copy of the "Story of My Life" handout.

Have them go through the timeline from "Birth" to "Present," listing all the extraordinary events that have happened to them so far. These events will be both good and bad. Some bad events may be painful for some students, like the death of a family member or friend. Be sensitive to these responses.

When everyone is finished, have those willing to share do so. If someone does not feel comfortable, that is OK.

ASK: Are you thankful for the ordinary, routine days?

ASK: Through these different events, where do you see God?

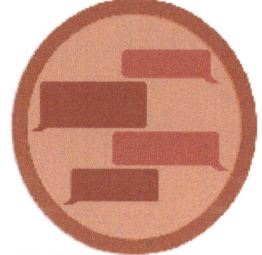

DISCUSSION QUESTIONS

OPTION 2: Show a clip from the beginning of the movie The Hobbit. The clip features Bilbo Baggins living a routine, ordinary life. He is completely fine until Gandalf and the dwarves show up. The scene starts with Bilbo eating supper and he gets a knock at his door. The scene ends when he opens the door and all the dwarves fall inside and Gandalf is standing outside looking in.

Here is a video clip you can use: https://www.youtube.com/watch?v=_LUPCclOULk
If you have the DVD, it starts at approximately 19:00
and goes to 23:15, on the extended version.

ASK: How do you react when your normal routine gets messed up?

ASK: When is a time that someone came along and messed up your plans?

ASK: When is a time that God messed up your plans? Of course by saying messed up, I mean that God changed your plans for something better.

NOW WHAT

NOW WHAT? (20 minutes)
SAY: In this last study of the Christian calendar, we are looking at what is called Ordinary Time. This is the time between Epiphany and Lent, and between Pentecost and Advent. There are no major holy days or seasons during Ordinary Time. Most of our church year, like real life, is spent in Ordinary Time. Christmas, Advent, Lent, and Easter each have their own seasons. Epiphany and Pentecost each have their own special days. In Ordinary Time, we celebrate and live in the days between those special seasons.

So does that mean that there are no special days in the church calendar during Ordinary Time? Of course not! Special days are made out of ordinary days.

Either in groups or individually, give students one of the following passages to look up:
Matthew 17:1-13 (Transfiguration Sunday), Matthew 3:13-17 (Baptism of Jesus), John 18:33-37 and Revelation 1:4-8 (Christ the King), Matthew 28:18-20 (Trinity Sunday), and Romans 12:1 (All Saints Day).

Read over the different special days of Ordinary Time with the students. This is found on pages 51-52. Ask each student to say which of these special days they think sounds best. Ask them why they like that particular day.

Give each student a notebook. It could be a regular sized notebook or a smaller one. These will be "Not So Ordinary Journals" for each to write in. Have them decorate their journals however they wish. Encourage your class to look for something extraordinary each day and write about it in their journal. Have them do this for a week to start with; if it goes well, extend it to two or three weeks, or longer. Encourage them to keep filling up pages with extraordinary things. They will be amazed that even on the most ordinary of days, they can find something extraordinary to write about.

LIVE IT

LIVE IT (5 minutes)
Close in a circle prayer. Going in the order of the alphabet, have each student name something ordinary that they are thankful for.

NOTES

Resources used in compiling background information: Liturgical Year: The Worship of God, The Westminster Dictionary of Theological Terms, https://www.youtube.com/watch?v=_LUPCclOULk, The Hobbit – The Unexpected Journey, 2012. Pictures used: TIME by Fabíola Medeiros - https://goo.gl/E3hmG7, Calendar* by Dafne Cholet - https://goo.gl/NH7WO3

STORY OF MY LIFE

SHARE YOUR LIFE'S TIMELINE BY WRITING OR DRAWING IMPORTANT EVENTS THAT HAVE HAPPENED ALONG THE WAY THESE EVENTS CAN BE BOTH GOOD AND BAD EXPERIENCES.

BIRTH DATE _____

PRESENT DAY

ABOUT THE AUTHORS

Andy McClung, a lifelong Cumberland Presbyterian, was ordained to the ministry of word and sacrament in 1995. He earned an Master of Divinity and Doctor of Ministry from Memphis Theological Seminary and has served churches in Alabama, Mississippi, Tennessee, and Arkansas. He now enjoys serving the CP Church on the presbytery, synod, and denominational levels. Andy lives in Memphis, Tennessee with his wife (also a CP minister) and their two children.

Jimmy Byrd is the pastor of New Hope Cumberland Presbyterian Church in Whitwell, Tennessee. He is married to Jennifer and has two sons, Daniel and Matthew. Jimmy has served in youth ministry for over 20 years in the Cumberland Presbyterian Church. He is a graduate of Bethel University and received his Master of Divinity at Memphis Theological Seminary.

www.ingramcontent.com/pod-product-compliance
Lightning Source LLC
Chambersburg PA
CBHW041426090426
42741CB00002B/51